You have never played music before or you cannot read sh
and inspiring hymns and spirituals. Don't worry! You will
pictured sheet music as simple as possible. You'll play by
or notes. The easy-to-play songs and melodies were adapt

The melodies have been transposed to one octave and simplified. Also, the number-coded notations
have been added and complex notations and symbols have been reduced. Such simplification
makes it possible for people to play melodies, especially those who can't read music or who have
never played music before.

The steel tongue drum and the handpan are percussion musical instruments designed to help you
focus on your feelings, sensations, and body. You don't need classical music training or
knowledge of music theory to play them. The primary purpose is relaxation, meditation, and traveling
through your inner world. No previous training or skills are necessary to enjoy these fascinating
instruments.

Play by Number

For tongue drums that have numbered musical notation, numbers 1 to 7 represent the keys
of the diatonic major scale. For example, a C Major scale would be:

1 = C (do)
2 = D (re)
3 = E (mi)
4 = F (fa)
5 = G (sol)
6 = A (la)
7 = B (ti / si)
8 (1̇) = C (do)

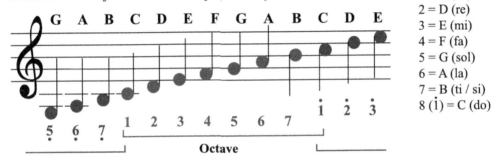

Dots above or below the numbers indicate a note from a
higher or lower octave, respectively.

Your drum can be numbered from 1 to 8, where 8 is note
C of the next octave. We use the number 1 with a dot
above the digit for this note because the most popular
models of tongue drums use this enumeration.

All songs in this book have been written with numbers
because most modern tongue drums have numbers
engraved or painted on their keys.

This book is aimed at those new to music and musical
instruments, whether child or adult. It allows for simple
and easy learning that requires no previous knowledge of
reading music.

Because most tongue drums include and are tuned to involve the notes of the main octave,
all songs from this book are possible to play in one octave.
If you have less than 1 octave of keys on your drum, you may need to skip some songs.
Each tongue drum is very different and it is impossible to accommodate songs for all kinds of
tongue drums in one book.

Contents

Amazing Grace

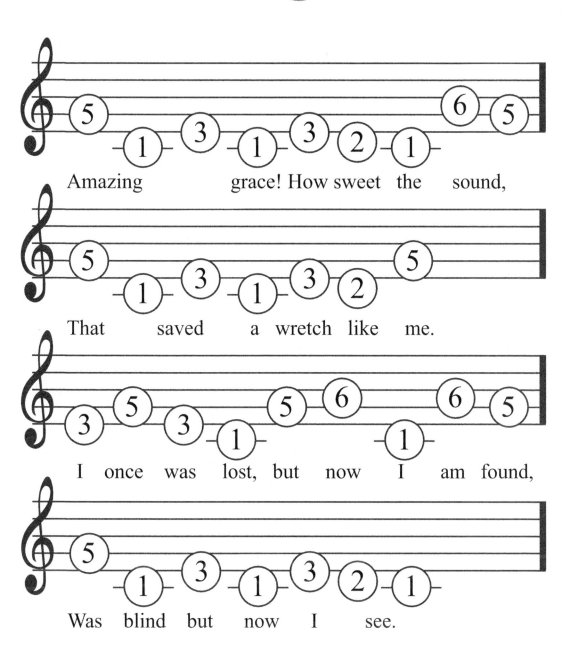

Amazing grace! How sweet the sound,

That saved a wretch like me.

I once was lost, but now I am found,

Was blind but now I see.

Was Grace that taught my heart to fear
And Grace, my fears relieved
How precious did that Grace appear
The hour I first believed

Through many dangers, toils and snares
We have already come
T'was Grace that brought us safe thus far
And Grace will lead us home
And Grace will lead us home

Amazing Grace, how sweet the sound
That saved a wretch like me
I once was lost but now am found
Was blind but now I see
Was blind, but now I see

Babylon's Falling

African-American Spiritual

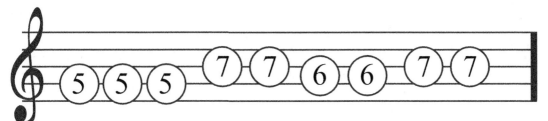

Ba - by - lon's   fal - ling, fal - ling,   fal - ling

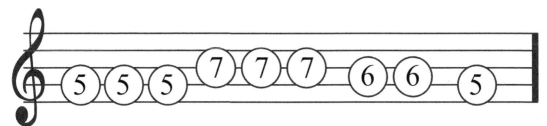

Ba - by - lon's fal - ling   to   rise   no   more.

Be Still My Soul

Katharina A. von Schlegel

3 2 3 4 3 2 3 1 2 2 3

Be still my soul the Lord is on thy side

3 2 3 4 3 2 3 1 2 3

Bear pa - tient - ly the cross of grief or pain

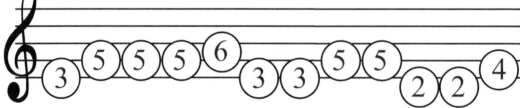

3 5 5 5 6 3 3 5 5 2 2 4

Leave to thy God to or - der and pro - vide

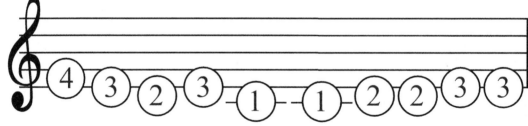

4 3 2 3 1 1 2 2 3 3

In ev - ery change He faith - ful will re - main

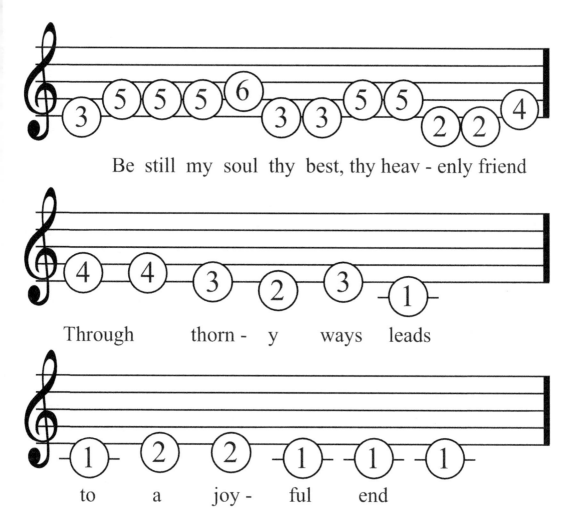

Be still, my soul, thy God doth undertake
To guide the future as He has the past
Thy hope, thy confidence let nothing shake
All now mysterious shall be bright at last
Be still, my soul, the waves and winds still know
His voice who ruled them while He dwelt below

Christ Was Born on Christmas Day

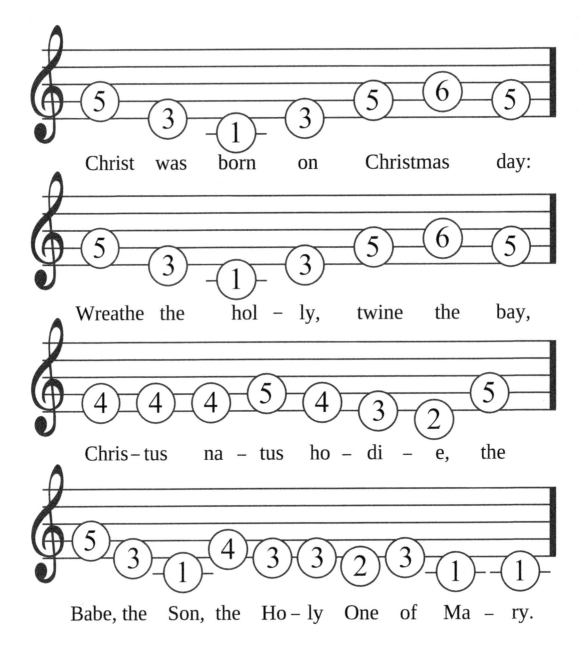

Christ was born on Christmas day:

Wreathe the hol – ly, twine the bay,

Chris – tus na – tus ho – di – e, the

Babe, the Son, the Ho – ly One of Ma – ry.

He is born to set us free,
He is born our Lord to be,
Ex Maria Virgine:
The God, the Lord, by all adored for ever.

Let the bright red berries glow
Ev'rywhere in goodly show:
Christus natus hodie:
The Babe, the Son, the Holy One of Mary.

Christians all, rejoice and sing,
'Tis the birthday of a King,
Ex Maria Virgine:
The God, the Lord, by all adored for ever.

Deck the Halls with Boughs of Holly

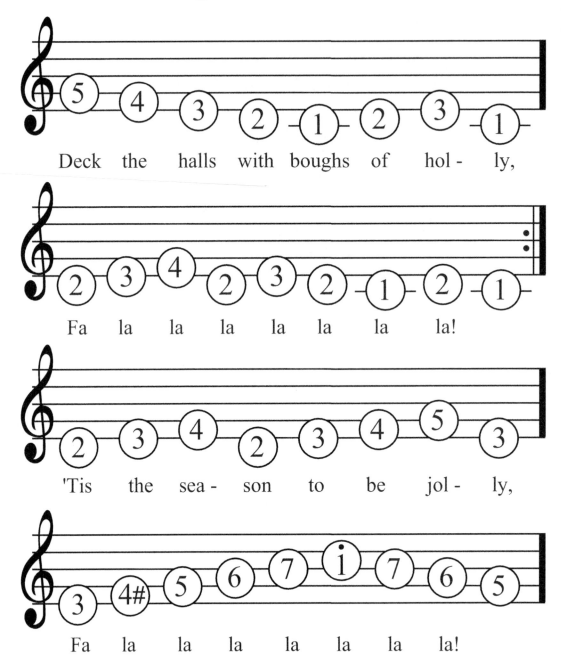

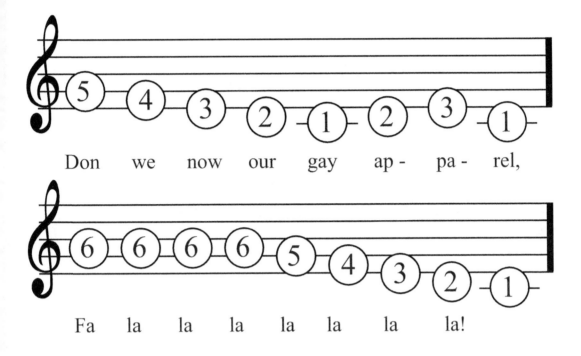

Don we now our gay ap - pa - rel,

Fa la la la la la la la!

Troll the ancient Yuletide carol, Fa la la la la la la la!

See the blazing yule before us, Fa la la la la la la la!
Strike the harp and join the chorus, Fa la la la la la la la!

Follow me in merry measure, Fa la la la la la la la!
While I tell of Yuletide treasure, Fa la la la la la la la!

Fast away the old year passes, Fa la la la la la la la!
Hail the new, ye lads and lasses, Fa la la la la la la la!
Sing we joyous all together! Fa la la la la la la la!
Heedless of the wind and weather, Fa la la la la la la la!

Elijah Rock

African-American Spiritual

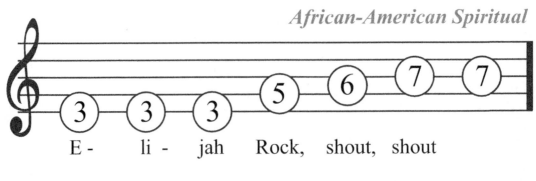

E - li - jah Rock, shout, shout

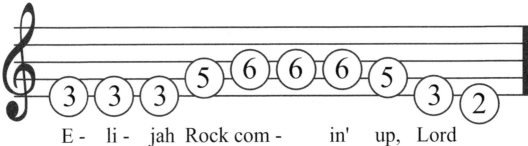

E - li - jah Rock com - in' up, Lord

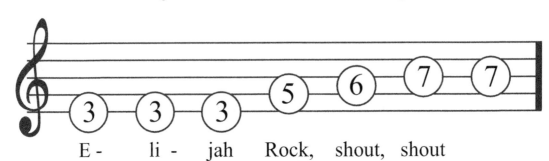

E - li - jah Rock, shout, shout

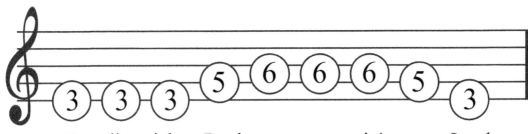

E - li - jah Rock com - in' up, Lord

Elijah, Elijah, Elijah
Elijah, Elijah, Elijah
Satan is a liar and a conjurer too
If you don't mind high, he'll come to you
If I could, I surely would
Stand on the rock where Moses stood
Elijah Rock, shout, shout, shout
Elijah Rock comin' up, Lord
Elijah Rock, shout, shout, shout
Elijah Rock comin' up, Lord
Ezekiel said he saw him
Wheel in the mid' of a wheel
John talked about him
In the book of the seven seals
Some say the Rose of Sharon
Others say the Prince of Peace
But I can tell this old world
He been a rock and a shelter for me
Hallelujah
Elijah Rock, shout, shout, shout
Elijah Rock comin' up, Lord
Elijah Rock, shout, shout, shout
Elijah Rock comin' up, Lord
You can call my rock in the morning
Call him late at night
He's always with me
And all my battles he'll fight
When I'm in trouble
I can call him on the line
He put a telephone in my heart
And I can call God anytime
Hallelujah

Elijah Rock, shout, shout, shout
Elijah Rock comin' up, Lord
Elijah Rock, shout, shout, shout
Elijah Rock I'm comin' up, Lord
You can call my rock in the morning
Call him late at night
He's always with me
All my battles he'll fight
When I'm in trouble
I can call him on the line
He got a telephone in my heart
And I can call God anytime
Hallelujah
Elijah Rock, shout, shout, shout
Elijah Rock comin' up, Lord
Elijah Rock, shout, shout, shout
Elijah Rock I'm comin' up, Lord

Every Time I Feel the Spirit

African-American Spiritual

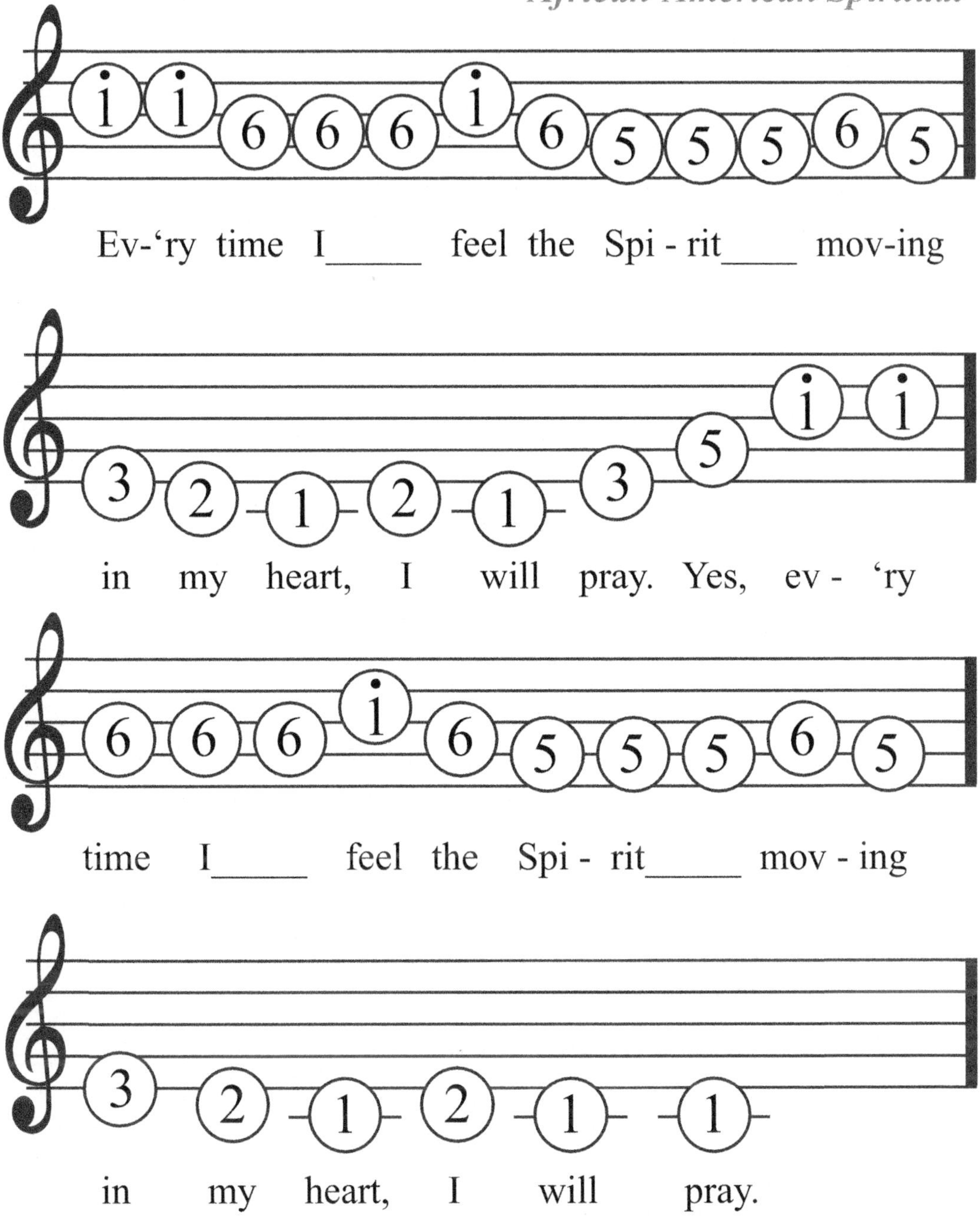

i i 6 6 6 i 6 5 5 5 6 5
Ev-‘ry time I_____ feel the Spi - rit____ mov-ing
3 2 1 2 1 3 5 i i
in my heart, I will pray. Yes, ev - ‘ry
6 6 6 i 6 5 5 5 6 5
time I_____ feel the Spi - rit_____ mov - ing
3 2 1 2 1 1
in my heart, I will pray.

God Is So Good

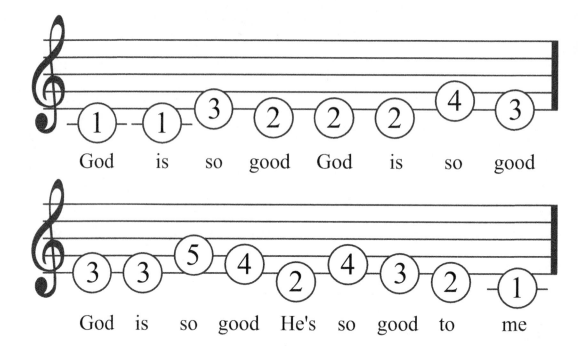

He cares for me
He cares for me
He cares for me
He is so good to me

I love him so Hallelujah
I love him so Hallelujah
I love his so Hallelujah
He is so good to me

God is so good
He's so good to me
God, You're so good
You're so good to me

Great Big Stars

African-American Spiritual

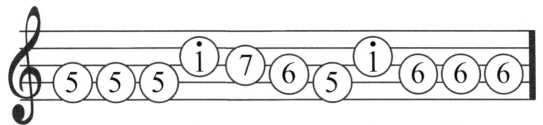

Great big stars, way ov - er yon - der Great big stars,

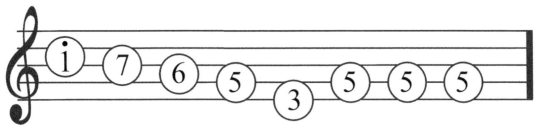

way ov - er yon - der Great big stars,

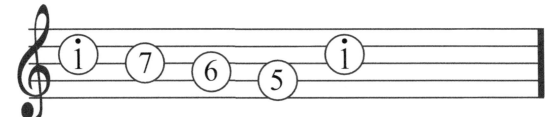

way ov - er yon - der.

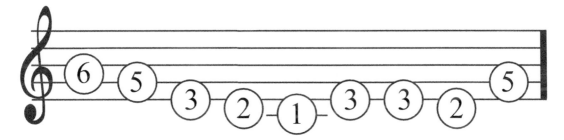

Oh, my lit - tle soul's going to shine, shine.

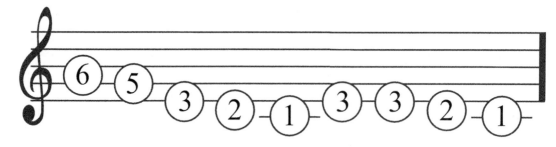

Oh, my lit - tle soul's going to shine, shine.

Star in the East, way up yonder,
Star in the East, way up yonder.
All around the world gonna shine, shine.
All around the world gonna shine, shine.

Great Day

African-American Spiritual

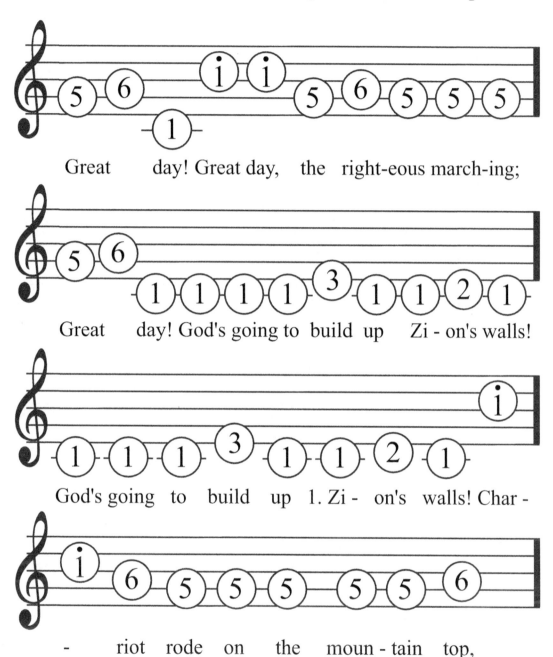

Great　　day! Great day,　the　right-eous march-ing;

Great　　day! God's going to　build　up　　Zi - on's walls!

God's going　to　　build　　up　1. Zi -　on's　walls! Char -

-　　riot　rode　on　　the　　moun - tain　top,

God's going to build up Zion's walls!

My God spoke and the char - iot did stop,

God's going to build up Zion's walls!

2 This is the day of jubilee,
God's going to build up Zion's walls!
The Lord has set His people free,
God's going to build up Zion's walls!
3 We want no cowards in our band,
God's going to build up Zion's walls!
We call for valiant-hearted men,
God's going to build up Zion's walls!
4 Goin't 'take my breastplate, sword and shield,
God's going to build up Zion's walls!
And march out boldly in the field,
God's going to build up Zion's walls!

He's Got the Whole World in His Hands

Traditional Spiritual

He's got the whole wide world

in his hands. He's got the whole world_____

in his hands. He's got the whole world_____

in his hands. He's got the wind and the rain

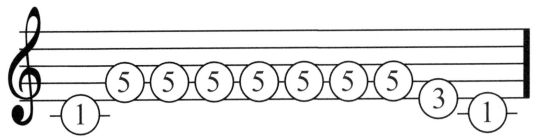

in his hands. He's got the wind and the rain

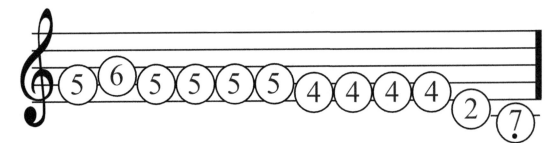

in his hands. He's got the wind and the rain

in his hands. He's got the wind and the rain

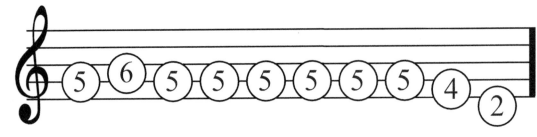

in his hands. He's got the whole world in his

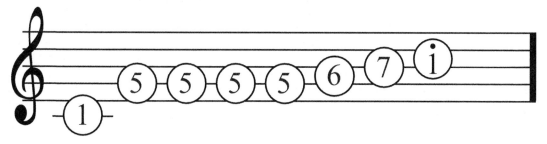

hands. He's got whole world in his hands.

He's got the little bitty baby in his hands.
He's got the little bitty baby in his hands.
He's got the little bitty baby in his hands.
He's got the whole world in his hands.

He's got you and me sister in his hands.
He's got you and me sister in his hands.
He's got you and me sister in his hands.
He's got the whole world in his hands.

He's got ev'rybody in his hands.
He's got ev'rybody in his hands.
He's got ev'rybody in his hands.
He's got the whole world in his hands.

Holy, Holy, Holy

Reginald Heber

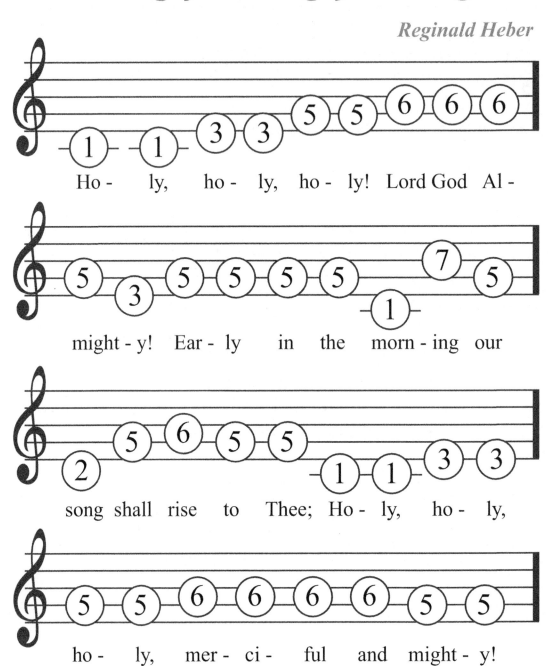

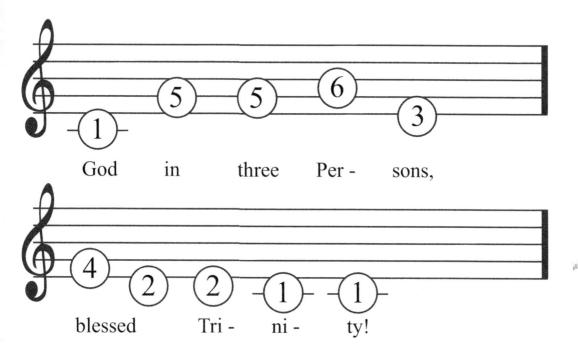

God in three Per - sons, blessed Tri - ni - ty!

Holy, holy, holy! All the saints adore Thee,
Casting down their golden crowns around the glassy sea;
Cherubim and seraphim falling down before Thee,
Who was, and is, and evermore shall be.

Holy, holy, holy! though the darkness hide Thee,
Through the eye of sinful man Thy glory may not see;
Only Thou art holy; there is none beside Thee,
Perfect in power, in love, and purity.

Holy, holy, holy! Lord God Almighty!
All Thy works shall praise Thy Name,
in earth, and sky, and sea;
Holy, holy, holy; merciful and mighty!
God in three Persons, blessed Trinity!

All the saints adore you
Laying crowns before You
Lifting praise unto You
You are holy, holy

All the angels bow down
Host of heaven cry out
With one voice with one sound
You are holy, holy

Peace Like a River

I've got love like an ocean (2 times)
I've got love like an ocean in my soul
I've got love like an ocean (2 times)
I've got love like an ocean in my soul

I've got joy like a fountain (2 times)
I've got joy like a fountain in my soul
I've got joy like a fountain (2 times)
I've got joy like a fountain in my soul

I've got peace, love and joy like a river (2 times)
I've got peace, love and joy like a river in my soul
I've got peace, love and joy like a river (2 times)
I've got peace, love and joy like a river in my soul

Jesus Loves Me

Anna Bartlett Warner, William B. Bradbury

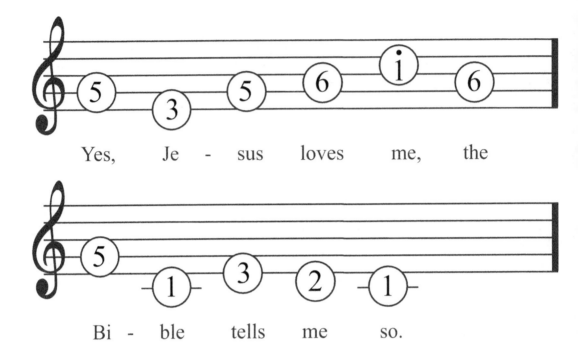

Jesus loves me, how can it be
That the only Son of God should care for me
To take away my sin and set me free
To take my life and make it all it's meant to be

Jesus loves me, this I know
It's not just the Bible that tells me so
I can feel it, feel it in my soul
Jesus loves me, this I know

Jesus loves me, he loves you too
You can't understand it all just believe it's true
He'll take away your old heart give you one that's new
You'll feel the walls come down
As His love comes breaking through

Jesus loves me, this I know
It's not just the Bible that tells me so
I can feel it, feel it in my soul
Jesus loves me, this I know

Jingle Bells

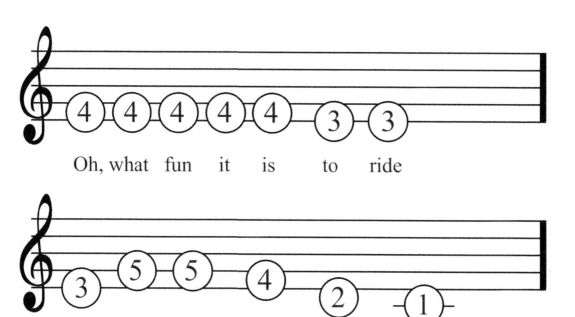

Oh, what fun it is to ride
in a one horse open sleigh.

Jolly Old Saint Nicholas

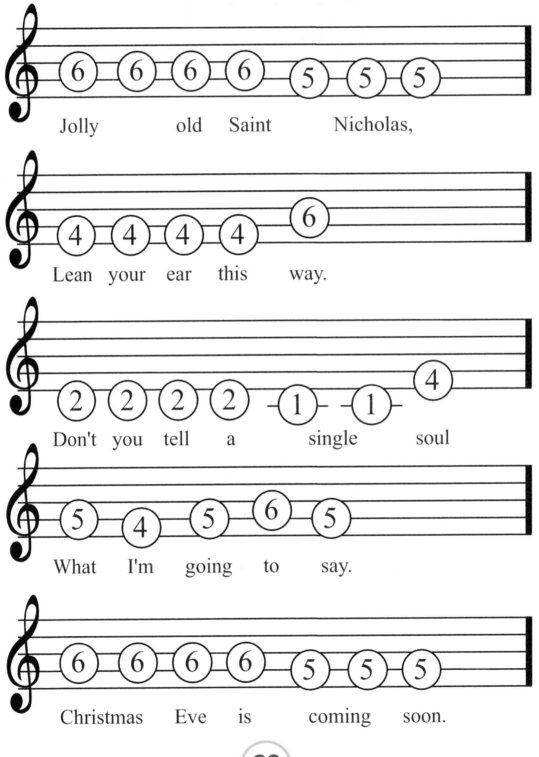

Joy to the World!

Isaac Watts, George Frederic Handel

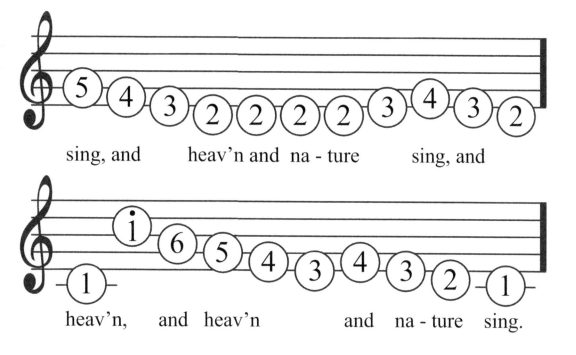

Joy to the earth, the Savior reigns!
Let men their songs employ,
while fields and floods, rocks, hills, and plains,
repeat the sounding joy,
repeat the sounding joy,
repeat, repeat the sounding joy

No more let sins and sorrows grow
nor thorns infest the ground;
he comes to make his blessings flow
far as the curse is found,
far as the curse is found,
far as, far as the curse is found

He rules the world with truth and grace
and makes the nations prove
the glories of his righteousness
and wonders of his love,
and wonders of his love,
and wonders, wonders of his love.

Just As I Am

Charlotte Elliott, William B. Bradbury

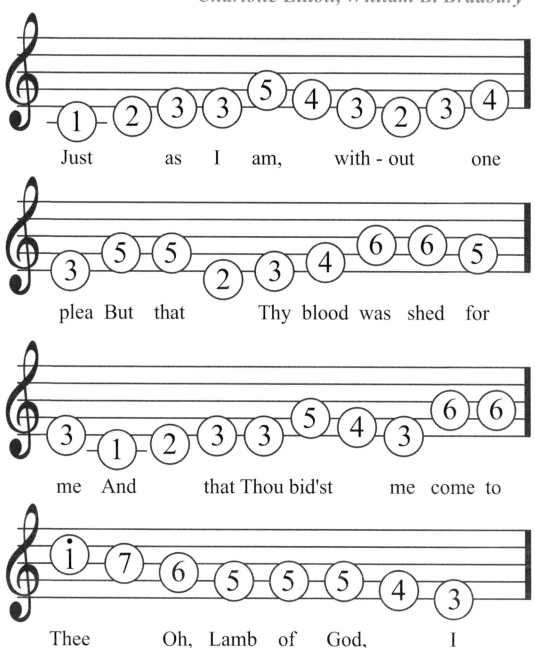

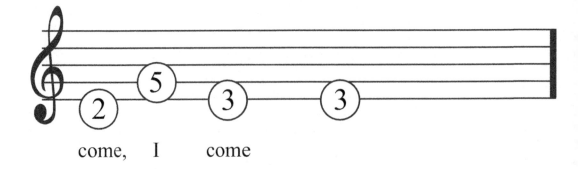

come, I come

Just as I am, though tossed about
With many a conflict, many a doubt,
Fighting and fears within without,
Oh, Lamb of God, I come, I come

Ooh, just as I am, ooh, I come
Ooh, just as I am, oh Lamb of God, I come

Just as I am, Thou wilt receive,
Wilt welcome, pardon, cleanse, relieve
Because Thy promise I believe,
Oh, Lamb of God, I come, I come

Ooh, just as I am, ooh, I come
Ooh, just as I am, oh Lamb of God, I come
Oh lamb of God, I come

Kumbaya, My Lord

African-American Spiritual

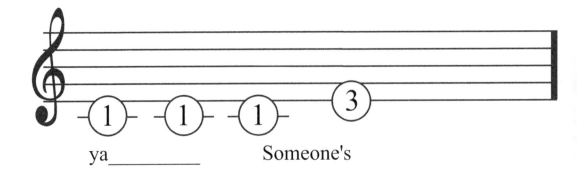

ya_____   Someone's

Singing Lord, kumbaya
Someone's singing Lord, kumbaya
Someone's singing Lord, kumbaya
Oh Lord, kumbayah

Someone's crying Lord, kumbaya
Someone's crying Lord, kumbaya
Someone's crying Lord, kumbaya
Oh Lord, kumbaya

Someone's praying Lord, kumbaya
Someone's praying Lord, kumbaya
Someone's praying Lord, kumbaya
Oh Lord, kumbaya

Oh Lord, kumbaya
Oh Lord, kumbaya
Oh Lord, kumbaya
Oh Lord, kumbaya

Michael Row
the Boat Ashore

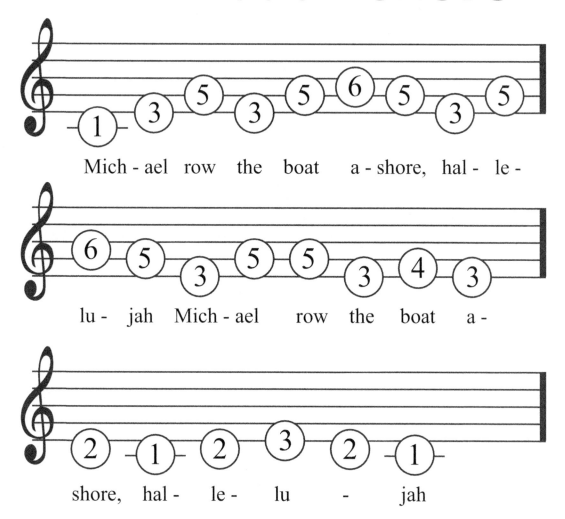

Mich - ael row the boat a - shore, hal - le -

lu - jah Mich - ael row the boat a -

shore, hal - le - lu - jah

Sister help to trim the sail, hallelujah
Sister help to trim the sail, hallelujah
The river is deep and the river is wide, hallelujah
Green pastures on the other side, hallelujah
Michael row the boat ashore, hallelujah
Michael row the boat ashore, hallelujah

Sister help to trim the sail, hallelujah
Sister help to trim the sail, hallelujah
Jordan's river is chilly and cold, hallelujah
Chills the body but not the soul, hallelujah
Michael row the boat ashore, hallelujah
Michael row the boat ashore, hallelujah
Sister help to trim the sail, hallelujah
Sister help to trim the sail, hallelujah
The river is deep and the river is wide, hallelujah
Milk and honey on the other side, hallelujah
Michael row the boat ashore, hallelujah
Michael row the boat ashore, hallelujah
Sister help to trim the sail, hallelujah
Sister help to trim the sail, hallelujah

O Sanctissima!

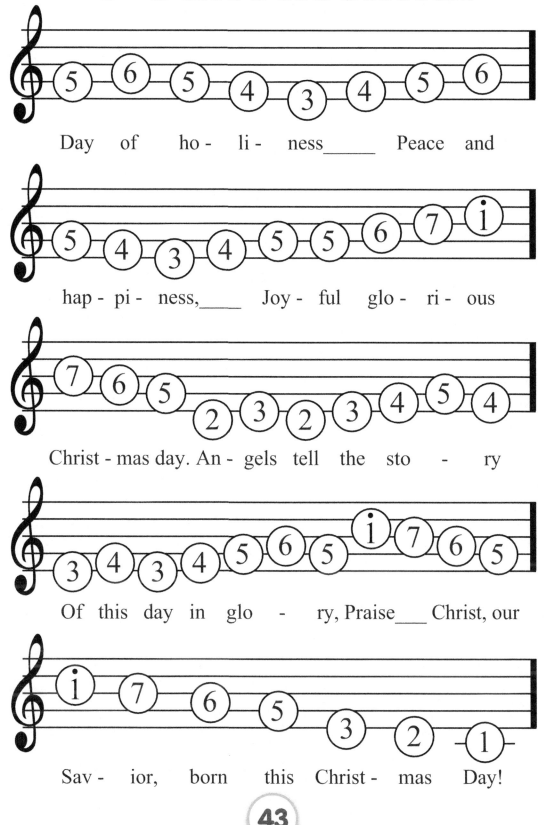

Praise Him, All You Little Children

Carey Bonner

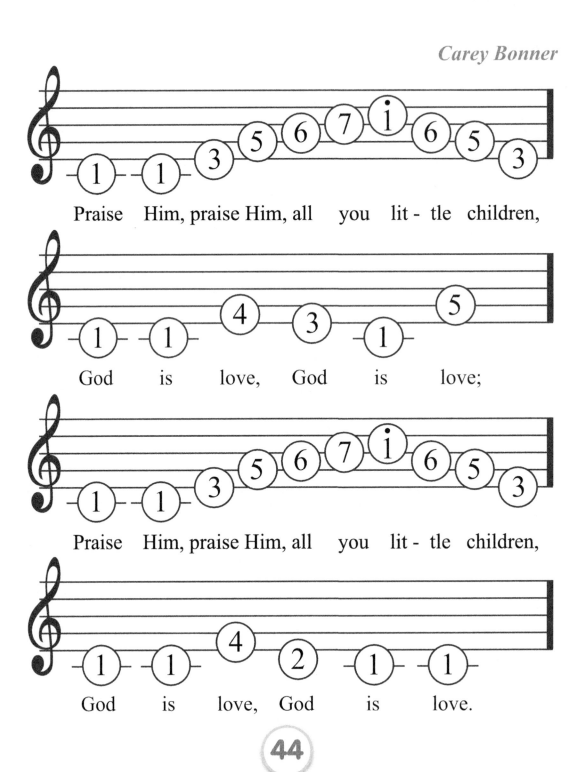

Praise Him, praise Him, all you lit - tle children,

God is love, God is love;

Praise Him, praise Him, all you lit - tle children,

God is love, God is love.

Love Him, love Him, all you little children,
God is love, God is love;
Love Him, love Him, all you little children,
God is love, God is love.

Thank Him, thank Him, all you little children,
God is love, God is love;
Thank Him, thank Him, all you little children,
God is love, God is love.

Shall We Gather at the River?

Robert Lowry

Shall we gather at the river?

Where bright angel feet have trod.

With its crystal tide for - ev - er flowing

by the throne of God.

Yes, we'll gather at the river the
beau - ti - ful, the beau - ti - ful river.
Gather with the saints at the river that
flows by the throne of God.

Soon we'll reach the shining river,
Soon our pilgrimage will cease,
Soon our happy hearts will quiver
With the melody of peace.
Yes, we'll gather at the river
The beautiful, the beautiful river
Gather with the saints at the river
That flows by the throne of God.

Silent Night, Holy Night

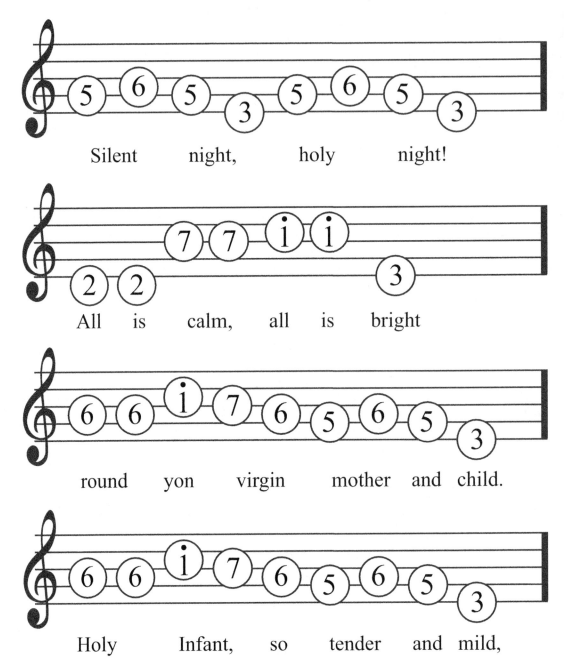

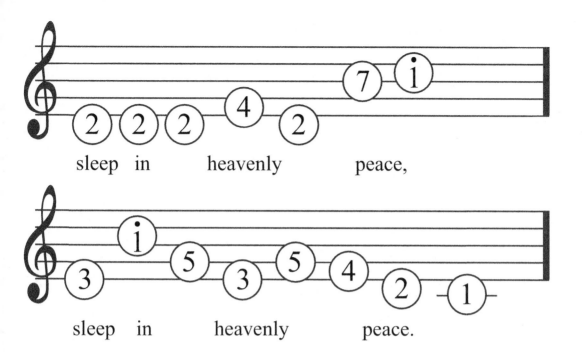

sleep in heavenly peace,

sleep in heavenly peace.

Silent night, holy night!
Shepherds quake at the sight.
Glories stream from heaven afar,
heav'nly hosts sing, Alleluia!
Christ, the Savior, is born!
Christ, the Savior, is born!

Silent night, holy night!
Son of God, love's pure light
radiant beams from thy holy face
with the dawn of redeeming grace,
Jesus, Lord, at thy birth,
Jesus, Lord, at thy birth.

Sinner Man

African-American Spiritual

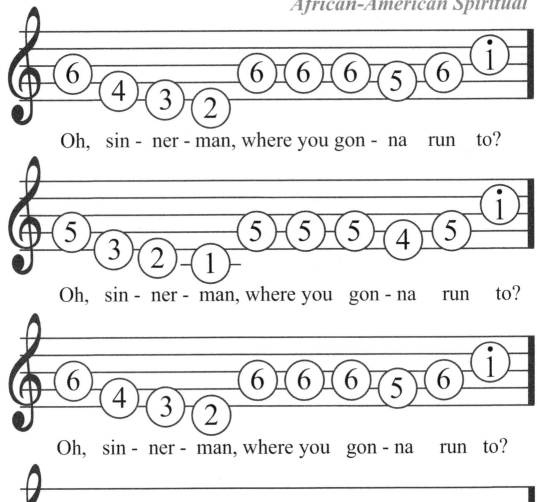

Oh, sin - ner - man, where you gon - na run to?

Oh, sin - ner - man, where you gon - na run to?

Oh, sin - ner - man, where you gon - na run to?

All on that day?

Run to the rock. Rock, won't you hide me? (3 times)
All on that day.
Run to the sea. Sea was a boilin' (3 times)
All on that day.
Oh, Sinnerman. Should-a been-a prayin' (3 times)
All on that day.

Am I a Soldier of the Cross

Isaac Watts

Must I be carried to the skies
On flow'ry beds of ease,
While others fought to win the prize
And sailed through bloody seas?

Are there no foes for me to face?
Must I not stem the flood?
Is this vile world a friend to grace,
To help me on to God?

Sure I must fight if I would reign:
Increase my courage, Lord;
I'll bear the toil, endure the pain,
Supported by Thy word.

Song of Praise

Richard Compton

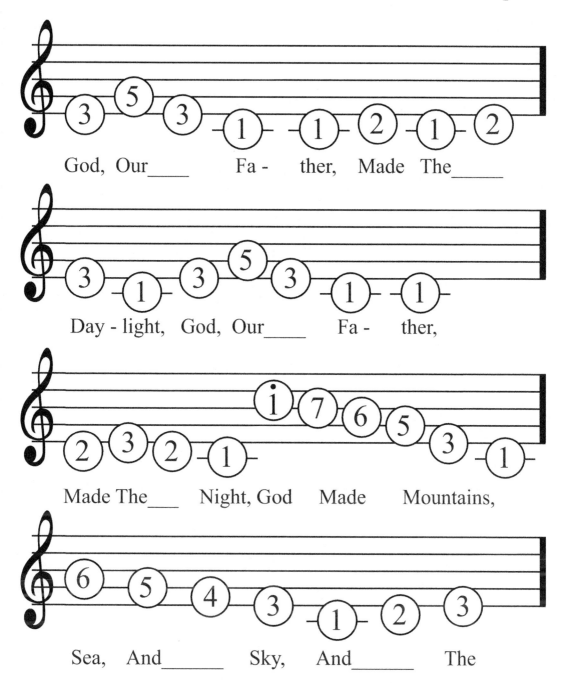

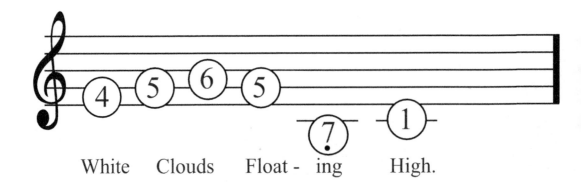

White   Clouds   Float - ing   High.

God, We Thank Thee For The Showers,
God, We Thank Thee For The Dew,
Mighty Trees And Flowers Small,
God, Our Father, Gave Them All.

The First Noel

The First Noel,

The Angels did say

Was to certain poor shepherds in fields where they lay,

In fields where they

Lay keeping their sheep

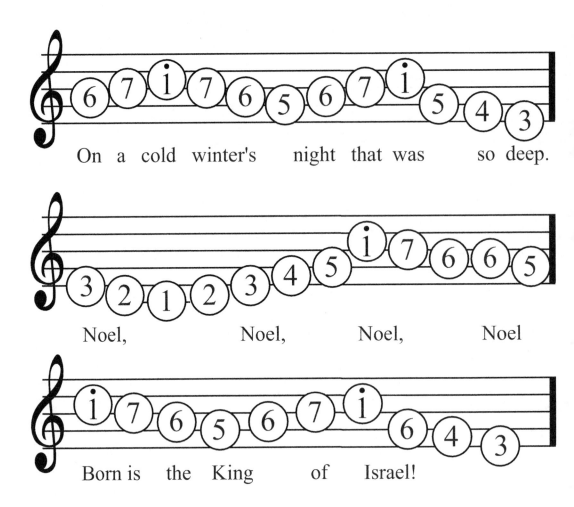

Twinkle,Twinkle Little Star

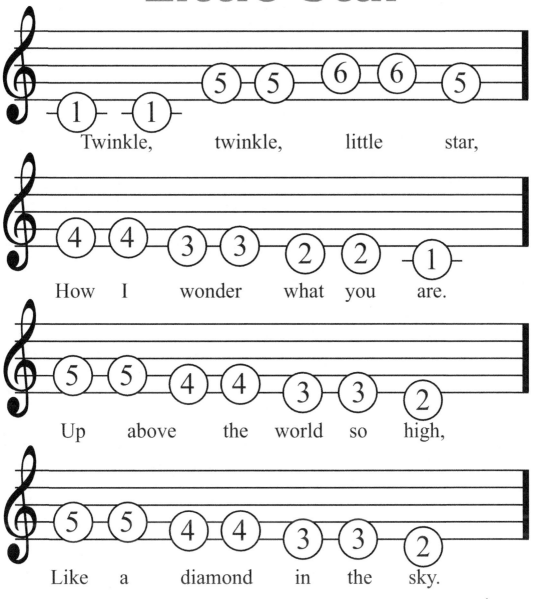

We Are Climbing Jacob's Ladder

African-American Spiritual

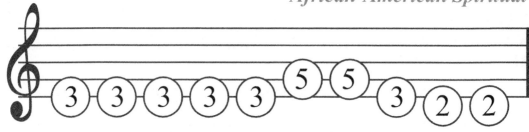

We are climb-ing Ja-cob's lad-der, We are

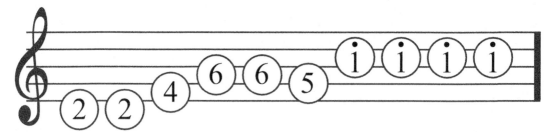

climb-ing Ja-cob's lad-der, We are climbing

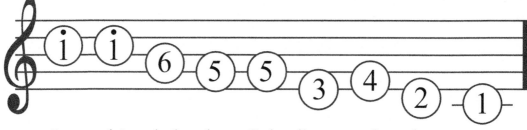

Ja-cob's lad-der, Sol-diers of the cross.

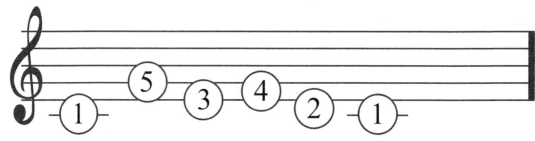

cross. Sol-diers of the cross.

Ev'ry round goes higher, higher,
Ev'ry round goes higher, higher,
Ev'ry round goes higher, higher,
Soldiers of the cross.

Children, do you love my Jesus?
Children, do you love my Jesus?
Children, do you love my Jesus?
Soldiers of the cross.

If you love Him, why not serve Him?
If you love Him, why not serve Him?
If you love Him, why not serve Him?
Soldiers of the cross.

Rise, shine, give God glory,
Rise, shine, give God glory,
Rise, shine, give God glory,
Soldiers of the cross.

We Are Marching (Siyahamba)

South-African Hymn

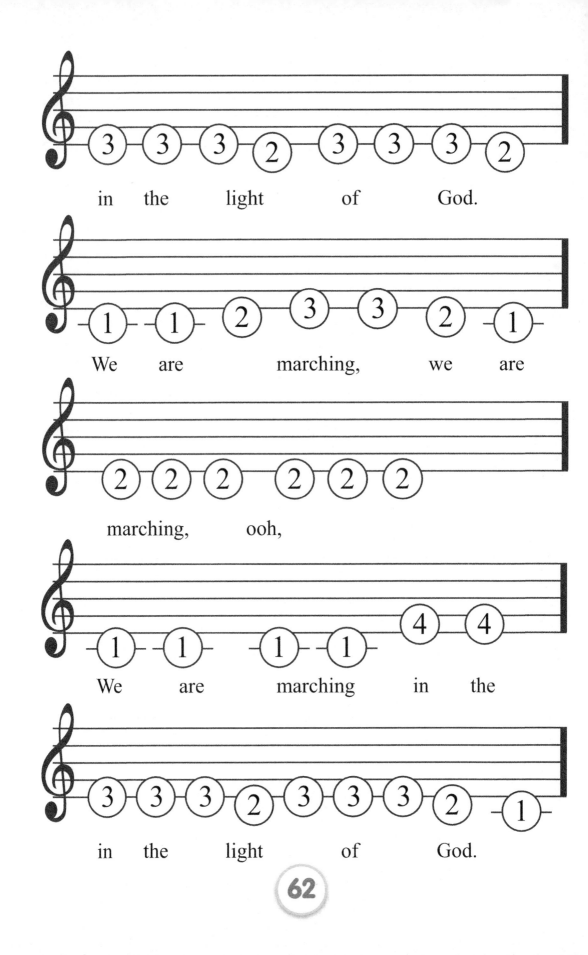

We Wish You a Merry Christmas

When the Saints Go Marchin' In

African-American Spiritual

And when the sun refuses to shine
When the sun refuses to shine
Lord, how I want to be in that number
When the Saints go marching in

Oh, when the Saints go marching in
Oh, when the Saints go marching in
Oh, how I want to be there on that morning
When the Saints go marching in

When the trumpet sounds its call
When the trumpet sounds its call
Oh, how I want be in that number
When the trumpet sounds its call

Oh, when the Saints go marching in
When the Saints go marching in
Lord, how I want to be in that number
Oh, when the Saints go marching in

Oh, when the new world is revealed
Oh, when the new world is revealed
Lord, how I want to be there on that morning
When the new world is revealed

Who Built the Ark?

African-American Spiritual

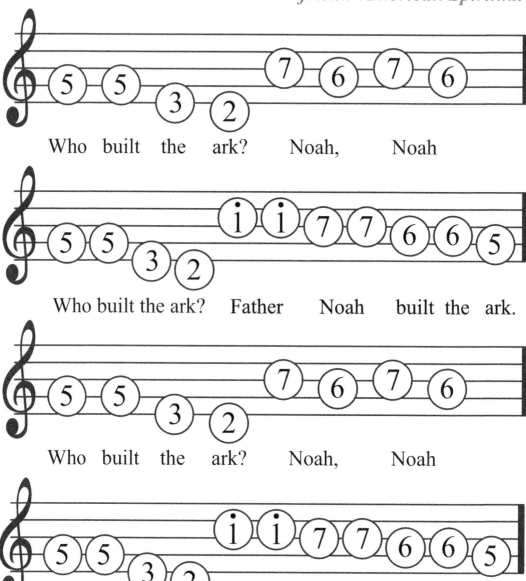

Old man Noah built the ark,____ he

built it out of___ a hick – o - ry bark.___

Built it long and wide and tall,____ with

plenty of room for the large and the small.__

Who built the ark?
Noah, Noah
Who built the ark?
Father Noah built the ark
In came the animals two by two
Hippopotamus and kangaroo
In came the animals three by three
Two big cats and a bumble bee
In came the animals four by four
Two through the window and two through the door
In came the animals five by five
Five little sparrows, doin' the jive
Who built the ark?
Noah, Noah
Who built the ark?
Father Noah built the ark
In came the animals six by six
The elephant laughed at the monkey's tricks
In came the animals seven by seven
Four from home and the rest from heaven
In came the animals eight by eight
Some were on time and the others were late
In came the animals nine by nine
Some were shoutin' and some were cryin'
In came the animals ten by ten
Five black roosters and five black hens
Now Noah says, "Go and shut that door
The rain's started dropping and we can't take more!"

Printed in Great Britain
by Amazon

44775540R00040